HUMAN COLLATERAL

Tanya Hilson

WELCOME PAGE

Hi, there reader ☺ Thank you for purchasing one of my works. Feel free to look into my other titles after you have completed this one. Enjoy!

- ✓ Ruby's Diner
- ✓ Back Porch Secrets
- ✓ Shadow Eyes
- ✓ Shadow Eye's 2 (Coming Soon)
- ✓ Back Porch Neighbors
- ✓ John's Hidden Truth
- ✓ My Cousin Sue

Remember to always Dream Big, for others cannot Dream for you.

Tanya Hilson

thisthatproduction.com

COPYRIGHT PAGE

TABLE OF CONTENTS

PROLOGUE

"No, we can't play together," Mill said as she shuffled a handful of cards. "The game is called Solitary, and you don't know how to play anyways." Mill and Remi were sitting at one of the tables in the deck area of the women's prison.

"Okay, can you teach me then?" Remi asked.

Mill studied the cards and did not answer. A corrections officer called out above the rowdy voices of inmates talking, laughing, and arguing. "Mill Brown! You have a visitor!"

"A visitor?" Remi teased. "You don't get visits. Who could it be? The president?"

Mill scowled as she got up. "Watch my cards," she said to Remi, who was still laughing.

The officer led Mill into a bright holding cell. The cell was empty but had a metal chair and a table in the center of the room. The metal of the chair reflected the lights from the fluorescent bulbs above. "Take a seat here," the officer said.

"I thought you said I had a visitor? Why are you putting me in the holding cell?" Mill asked.

The officer turned and walked out, leaving Mill standing by the chair.

"What the fuck is going on? Why the hell do they got me up in here?" Mill shouted at the officer.

A moment later, the door opened again, and two men dressed in dark suits walked in.

"Ms. Brown," the first man said.

"Who the hell are you?" Mill replied.

"Hi Mill," said the second man. "Do you remember me?"

Mill looked at him. "Yeah, I remember you, Agent Shaw. What the fuck do you want?" she asked, gripping the backrest of the chair. "Why are you here? I haven't done shit. And if this is about that bitch Banks, she attacked me!"

"No, this is not about some prison yard scuffle," Agent Shaw replied. "Please take a seat."

Mill sat down and crossed her legs.

"This is Agent Porter," Shaw said. Mill glared at him but did not say anything.

"We would like to talk to you in regards to DCFS."

"What about DCFS? What the hell does DCFS have to do with me being in here with you two?" Mill tapped her foot as she talked.

"I'm not a detective anymore, Ms. Brown."

"Oh? I meant Mr. FBI Agent." Mill said sarcastically.

"Do you want to hear me out or not?"

"What is this about, and why are you asking me about DCFS?"

Agent Porter was holding a cream-colored file in one hand. His other hand hung loosely in his pants pocket as he handed Mill a file.

"Oh! So, what the hell do the FBI want with me?" Mill said, taking the file from him and holding it unopened.

"Do you recognize any of those people in the file?"

"Will I get time taken off my sentence if I agree with whatever this is?"

"Please look at the pictures, ma'am," Shaw asked.

Mill opened the file and studied it. In an instant, her forehead furrowed in recognition. The agents watched her intently.

"Dr. Kook?" she said

"How do you know Dr. Kook?" Agent Porter leaned forward.

"He's one of the doctors at the Woodlawn clinic." Mill continued to flip through the photos. "And this is...." She stopped flipping, and her eyes widened in horror. "Oh my God!" Mill looking shocked. "What happened? I had nothing to do with this!"

PART ONE

(Two Years Earlier)

CHAPTER ONE

A loud banging on Mill's Chicago apartment door startled her, and the baby in the rocker began to cry. Mill hurried out of her bedroom, a bottle of milk in her hand. She mumbled under her breath as she picked the baby up, feeding her the bottle.

"Who the hell knocking on my door like that?" In one corner of the sitting room, a 32-inch TV sat on four orange crates. It looked like it could fall off at any moment. A toddler sat in a high chair across from the TV, watching Sesame Street and eating dry Cheerios. Mill walked to the door, rocking her crying daughter, and looked through the peephole. She frowned, confused, and took one step back from the door.

"Who the hell knocking on my door like the police?" she asked.

A woman's muffled voice came through the door. "Hello, I'm looking for a Millicent Brown?"

"And who are you?"

"My name is Dae Ross. I'm with the Department of Children and Family Services." Mrs. Ross pulled out her badge and held it close to the peephole for Mill to see.

"What the hell DCFS doing at my door?"

"If you open the door and let me in, I can explain why I'm here, Ms. Brown," Mrs. Ross said as she tucked the badge back in her pocket.

"You can explain through the door. How do I know if that badge or ID is even real? And why would DCFS be at my door? I haven't done anything wrong."

"Do you want me to keep talking through the door? I can call the police if you don't open up this door, Ms. Brown."

Mill opened the door, and Mrs. Ross entered. It was daytime, but inside, the apartment was dim, and the windows were closed. Empty food containers littered a black folding table in the middle of the room, and a trash can in the corner overflowed.

"Thank you," Mrs. Ross said as she entered the apartment. She was shorter than Mill and had an authoritative, powerful persona about herself. A small purse hung from her shoulder as she held a clipboard of papers in her hand. She pressed her lips tightly together as she took in the disarray of Mill's apartment.

"You say your name is Mrs. Ross? I never heard of a Chinese person having the last name Ross. Can I see your ID again?"

"I hear that a lot," Mrs. Ross said as she pulled out the badge and ID once again, showing it to Mill, who looked at it, passing it back to Mrs. Ross. "My husband is African-American. And I'm Korean, not Chinese."

"So you're looking to talk to me for what?" Mill asked as she walked back to the table, taking a seat. The baby had quieted down, drinking from the bottle.

"The Department of Children and Family Services received an anonymous call saying your children are not being taken care of and you leave them alone at times."

"A call! A call from who? I do take care of my children. I don't know why somebody would call and tell you all some shit like that."

"I'm sure it was just somebody concerned about the children. May I have a seat, Ms. Brown?" Mrs. Ross smiled tightly.

Mill gestured at the chair in front of her.

"As I was saying," Mrs. Ross said, taking the seat, "someone called complaining that they hear your babies crying all day and night. We were also told that you have a substance abuse problem, and you leave your kids in the house alone to go buy drugs. People are concerned your children are being neglected."

Mill had stopped feeding the baby. She got up, placed her in the swing beside the black couch, and gave it a slight push. She then walked over to the high chair, picked up the toddler, and put him on her lap. "I don't know who's spreading those lies," she said, "hell, all babies cry. As you can see, my baby girl was crying when you walked in, and now she's lying there quiet, swinging in her swing. Babies cry!"

"Yes, babies do cry," Mrs. Ross said.

Mill pulled at the waistband of the toddler's pull-up and peeked inside. "And as far as me neglecting them, that's a whole lie." She grabbed a new pull-up from a diaper bag, moved the empty food containers off the table, and started changing the toddler. "I feed my son. And my daughter is still on formula, which I get from the WIC store. Do you see neglect?"

"No need to get defensive, ma'am," Mrs. Ross replied. "I'm just here to do my job and get some information." She started writing on the notepad attached to the clipboard. "What are your children's names, Ms. Brown? And their ages?"

Mill leaned forward to see what was being written in the notepad, and Mrs. Ross, noticing this, angled the pad away from her.

"My son's name is Darius, and he's almost two," Mill said.

"And your daughter?" Mrs. Ross asked. Mill noticed that Mrs. Ross had scribbled more than just Darius' name and age onto the notepad. "My daughter's name is Jayden, and she's five months." She folded up the dirty pull-up and set it on the table.

"And their father? Is he around?"

"No, they're not," Mill said, bouncing Darius on her lap and looking over at Jayden, who was starting to fall asleep. "It's just us."

"Are you receiving any child support from their fathers?"

"Does it look like I'm receiving anything from them niggas? I take care of my kids by myself."

"And do you work, Ms. Brown?"

"Taking care of them is a job, Mrs. Ross."

"That's a no?" Mrs. Ross said, sitting up straighter in her chair and scribbling furiously into the notepad. "Do your children have a primary doctor you take them to see? If so, when was the last time you took them in?"

"I take them up the street to the Woodlawn Health Center. My kids just recently had check-ups."

Mill got up and placed Darius back in the high chair. She gave him a bottle of apple juice before saying, "Again, I don't know why somebody would call your office, telling y'all bullshit." She walked back to the swing, took a small pillow, and used it to support her daughter's head.

"Sorry if it seems like I'm asking a lot of questions," Mrs. Ross stated, "but it's part of the job. Now, are you on any drugs, Ms. Brown? Anything that your doctor does not prescribe?"

"Look, lady..." Mill started saying.

"It's Mrs. Ross."

"Look, Mrs. Ross, I may look skinny, but I eat like a horse, and I keep food in the house not only to feed my kids but to feed myself too." She walked over to the kitchen and flung open the cabinets and refrigerator. "As you can see, Mrs. Ross, I keep food."

Mrs. Ross nodded and pressed her lips even tighter. She tapped her pen against the clipboard. "I see the food Ms. Brown, but you never answered my question."

"You asked a lot of questions." Mill picked up a pack of Newport cigarettes lying on top of the refrigerator and took one out. She lit it on the stove and took a long, deep drag before walking back to the table. Blowing the smoke out of her mouth, she asked, "Which question?"

"Are you on any drugs, Ms. Brown? Anything that your doctor does not prescribe?"

Mill looked at Mrs. Ross through the thick fog of cigarette smoke now hanging between them. Mrs. Ross fanned her free hand in front of her face to clear out the smoke. "Would it be okay if you cracked a window?" She asked. "Plus, smoke is not good around kids, especially a newborn."

Mill leaned forward and locked eyes with her. "Are you telling me I can't smoke in my own damn house where I pay the bills, Mrs. Ross?"

"Disrespectful bitch!" Mrs. Ross cursed under her breath.

"What you say?"

"I'm going to ask you again, Ms. Brown, are you on any drugs? Anything that your doctor does not prescribe?"

"If you consider dope dick a drug, then yes, I'm on it. You should know what black dick feels like. You say your husband is black – no, wait, I meant African-American."

Sharp frown lines appeared between Mrs. Ross's brows as she wrote on the notepad. She was irritated by Mill's attitude and the cigarette smoke. The filth and airlessness of the apartment made her headache. "If you keep avoiding the question, I'm going to assume you are doing drugs."

"No! I'm not on drugs. The only drugs I take are Tylenol, and that's when I'm cramping or have a headache."

"The allegations against you are serious. I still have to look around your house as a precaution, and I will need to see both of your children's papers from their primary doctor. I would also need the doctor's name who you and your children see at the Woodlawn Health Center."

"And what do you need all that for?" Mill asked as Mrs. Ross started to gather her things into her purse. "I'll have to look for their papers."

"You are receiving government assistance, so DCFS has the right to make sure that these children are okay."

"I can show you around the apartment, but I will have to look for the papers from the doctor's office."

"I will need to see their shot records too."

"I will find what I can," Mill looking irritated.

Moments later, Mrs. Ross and Mill returned from looking around the apartment. They sat back at the table.

"Ms. Brown, I do not know if you leave your children alone, but I do know that DCFS will be keeping an eye on you to make sure these children are being taken care of properly. I will be back here in a few days to get the paperwork from your doctor's office and to make sure you clean up around here. This apartment is mucky."

"What the hell is mucky?"

"It could use a nice cleaning," Mrs. Ross answered.

Mill picked up a broom that had been leaning against the couch and started sweeping the floor. "Look, Mrs. Ross, I had some company over. As a matter of fact, I was about to clean up before you got here. It's never like this."

"There's one more thing I need to do before I go," Mrs. Ross said. Mill stood motionless, the broom still in her hand. "I need to look your children over."

Mill let the broom go, and it fell against the wall. She grabbed Darius out of his high chair and sat down with him at the table. "I don't abuse my kids, lady... I mean, Mrs. Ross."

"Again, Ms. Brown, this is normal procedure when agents are sent out to homes to investigate any allegations of abuse or neglect."

Mill watched as Mrs. Ross inspected her children. Mrs. Ross's face was unreadable, and her manner was brisk and emotionless. She examined the children thoroughly, looking for bruises and marks. Mill put Darius back in his high chair with his apple juice and dry Cheerios when she finished.

"As I said, I don't abuse my children," Mill repeated.

"The children look fine, but I will be back in a few days. If your children are being left alone, or we find that you are on drugs, your children will be placed into DCFS custody. DCFS takes these things seriously."

Mrs. Ross walked towards the front door, and Mill followed behind her. Mrs. Ross was standing outside the door now. "Enjoy your evening, and make sure you clean this place up. A dirty apartment can be a sign of neglect, too."

With this, she turned and left. Mill slammed the door leaning against it as Jayden began to cry again.

CHAPTER TWO

M ill sat at her table, smoking a cigarette. The apartment was quiet, and her children were sleeping inside her bedroom. She puffed nervously as she spoke on her cell phone.

"Look, I ain't trying to hear this shit right now, Mill, I'm about to bring some blow over, and we're having a few johns and girls over too," Lou said.

"Did you hear me nigga? I said that DCFS is watching me now. Somebody called them saying I be leaving the kids in the house by themselves, and she wants to see their vaccination records from the doctor." Her right leg was shaking. "She said she'd be back in a few days, so ain't none of that trap shit tonight or this week. Nigga, if they take my kids, then what the fuck am I going to do? Section 8 pays this rent, not you." Mill's hand was unsteady as she tapped off the ash from her cigarette into the ashtray. She looked around the room with worry on her face.

"Stop being on that scary shit," Lou said. "It's Friday, and motherfuckers got them checks. We getting this money tonight, and you know your ass need the bread. I'm on my way!" Lou hung up with a sharp click, and Mill stood up and paced the floor.

She sat back down and thought to herself, 'now, who the hell is all up in my business? I bet it's that damn nosey-ass church lady.' She blew cigarette smoke through her nostrils. 'I'm going to give her nosey-ass a piece of my mind.' She smashed the cigarette tip into the ashtray and walked out of her apartment across the hall to her neighbor's unit. She paused and then knocked hard on the door. "Open this door, old lady. It's me, Mill. I know your nosey ass hear me knocking."

"What you knocking at my door for?" the neighbor cracked her door open with the chain still attached, peeping at Mill. "Ain't no dope over here," she said.

Mill stared at the old woman through the chained door. "I know it was your old ass that called DCFS on me. See, everybody else scared to give you a piece of their mind, but I'm going to give you a piece of mine."

"Child, get away from my door."

"Stay the hell out of my business before your ass end up falling down the stairs, if you know what I mean."

"Is that a threat?" Ms. Betty replied.

"Try me, old lady."

"You need to be tending to your kids instead of being at my door."

"Stay the fuck out of my business with your old cripple-face ass!" Mill yelled as Ms. Betty slammed her door shut.

* * *

Later that night, Mill and Lou sat together at the folding table, portioning out dope onto tiny pieces of foil, folding the foil up, and placing them into small plastic baggies.

"How that shit is?" Lou asked.

Mill took a rolled-up dollar bill and snorted a line of blow through it. She wiped her nose, leaned her head back, and her face relaxed with a smile. "This some good shit," she said as she wiped her nose.

"I told you, you'll like this shit. Help me finish bagging this dope so we can get this money. And let me get that dollar bill too, so I can hit the shit."

"Yeah, I need this money, I have shit to buy for my kids, and I need to get my nails and hair done too." She stood up and walked towards the room where her children were sleeping. "Let me check on my kids and remember, my room is off-limits to the fucking and sucking," she warned, "my children will be in there."

"No shit! The door is going to be closed and locked. I got my shit up in there too." Lou snorted another line of dope and walked over to the refrigerator, where he pulled out a fifth of Hennessey. He looked at his phone. "Cool, Bam, just text me and said he's on his way."

"There's something about that yellow nigga Bam I don't like." Mill walked into the kitchen, grabbing the Hennessey and pouring herself a drink.

"Ain't no need to be worrying about Bam," Lou said, "Bam knows I will fuck him up if he tries anything."

"I just don't trust dude. I see jealousy in that nigga eyes every time he comes around. Remember, there are some back-stabbing-ass motherfuckers out here in these streets, Lou. You can't trust everybody."

Lou lightly grinned to himself. "If that nigga or any other nigga try to pull some shit with me...." Lou paused and pulled out a gun from the back of his pants. "Rock-a-bye, baby,"

* * *

Mill was at the table the following day, feeding Darius oatmeal as he sat in his high chair.

"We made some good money last night," she said to Lou.

"I told your scary ass we were going to get this bread." Lou pulled out a green apple Royal Crown bag full of cash and placed it on the table. He passed Mill a roll of money. "Here's your cut."

Mill looked the money over. "Yeah, we did real good." She counted the bills as her smile got bigger.

"I'm about to cut out," Lou said as he stood up from the table.

Suddenly, Mill heard two loud knocks at the door. The knocks were so hard that the door nearly came off the hinges. "CHICAGO PD!" Shouted a man on the other side of the door. With a loud BOOM! The door flew open, and splinters from the doorframe flew in all directions. Mill barely had time to comprehend what was happening when a SWAT team in full tactical gear barged in.

"Get down!" The first officer shouted.

"What the hell?" Mill looking shocked.

"Clear!" Said the second officer.

"Let me see your hands!" Detective Romano commanded, grabbing Lou and throwing him up against the wall.

During the chaos, Detective Shaw entered the apartment. He was wearing a windbreaker. "Millicent Brown," he said, "we have a warrant to search your apartment."

"A warrant? A warrant for what?"

The children had started crying.

"What's going on?" Mill asked, her voice shaky.

Detective Romano approached Mill from behind and yanked her arms behind her back. Mill gasped in pain as Romano placed handcuffs on her wrists.

"Please, loosen these cuffs. They're too tight," Mill begged.

"Get used to it," Romano responded.

"Have a seat on the couch, Ms. Brown," said Detective Shaw.

"What the hell is this all about?" Mill asked. She fidgeted in her handcuffs.

"Don't act fucking dumb," Detective Romano responded, "you know why the fuck we're here, doesn't she, Mr. Louis Epps?"

Mill shot Lou a confused and angry look.

"Nah, I don't know what the fuck you talking about, detective," Lou said as he mean mugged Romano.

"Did y'all really think you could get away with running a trap house in my city?" Detective Romano asked them. "I have eyes everywhere."

A young man came walking in through the front door. He was wearing a matching windbreaker and bulletproof vest. Lou looked up at him, and his eyes narrowed in recognition. "Bam? Nigga, you a narc? Motherfuckers said something wasn't right with your yellow ass!"

"I told you something wasn't right with that nigga..."

Detective Shaw walked in from the bedroom, holding a plastic bag. Now, look what we have here." He dumped the bag's contents onto the table displaying drugs, two nine-millimeter handguns, and rolled up money.

Mill looked at Lou with a frown, then up at the Detectives.

"Ms. Brown," Detective Shaw said, "so, you still saying that you don't know why we're here? Whose shit is this then? Yours or Lou's?"

"I don't know anything about no guns, drugs, or a damn trap house. I just came over here to visit and get some ass."

Mill looked at Lou in shock."Y'all planted that shit. That shit wasn't back there."

"Ain't nobody plant shit," Bam intervened, "I got both of you on video selling drugs and pussy up in here."

"Narc-ass Nigga," Lou spat out at Bam.

A swat officer pulled Lou to his feet. Detective Romano asked the officer to take Lou out to the squad car. "Don't forget to read him his rights," he reminded the officer.

Mill watched with her heart beating fast as the officer walked a kicking and struggling Lou out to the squad car.

"Regardless whose shit this is," Detective Romano places the evidence back into the plastic bag, "both of you are going to jail."

Mill curled up her lips at Detective Romano, and tears started to well up in her eyes.

"Going to jail? What about my kids?" She asked.

"Were you thinking about your kids when you were selling drugs and ass out of here?" Romano said as a female officer grabbed Mill by the arm and pulled her up from the couch. Tears flowed down her face.

"DCFS is here," Bam called out.

"You yellow-ass narc nigga...." Mill said.

Mrs. Ross was standing in the doorway. "I told you I'd be back, and here we are. It hasn't been twenty-four hours, and the police are knocking down your door already." She shook her head in disbelief as she looked into Mill's eyes.

"Leave my kids alone! Where are you taking them? Somebody say something! Wait, my neighbor Ms. Betty from across the hall, she can get my kids!" Mill shouted.

Mrs. Ross walked to the highchair and picked Darius up. Then she picked up Jayden, who had been in the rocker. "It's okay, babies, I'll take care of you from here." Mill tried to tug away from the officer as she watched Mrs. Ross carry her children away.

"My kids!" she cried. "Where are you taking my kids?!"

CHAPTER THREE

M rs. Ross walked into the DCFS facility carrying Mill's children. "Good afternoon, Mr. Fluke," she said to the nerdy-looking man sitting at a desk. "We have two children here, a boy named Darius and his sister Jayden."

Danny Fluke (aka Mrs. Ross's flunky) looked up from his computer just as Mrs. Ross passed Darius to him. "Oh, hello there, Lil man!" He said to Darius. Mrs. Ross laid Jayden down into the playpen beside her desk.

"The children have been taken to the hospital and given exams," she said. "Both are healthy."

Danny bounced Darius up and down on his knee and handed him a teddy bear. "Lord knows we don't need any more dope fiend babies coming up in here. It's hard to get rid of dope fiend babies."

"Call upstairs and make preparations for these children to be housed." She poured herself a cup of coffee from the coffee maker.

"With the looks of things, their mother will be going to jail for a very long time." She sipped her coffee and looked down at Jayden in the playpen as Danny placed Darius in the playpen with his sister.

Mrs. Ross walked back to her desk and sat down. "These children are young. We should have no problem getting a lot of money for them." She smiled and sipped her coffee. "It's rare that we get an infant and a toddler with no drugs in their system."

"Damn, that might help the mother's case," Danny said.

"Nah! The doctor we're paying will say that the baby girl had some drugs in her system. Also, Detective Romano is putting the charges together as we speak."

Danny leaned back on his chair, kicked his feet up on the desk, and clasped his hands behind his neck. "Well, if *Romano* is on it, then we won't have to worry about their mother getting out anytime soon. So, how much are you paying him?"

She looked up at Danny with a sinister smile. "It's rude to ask about another man's money. Once their mother receives her time, we can start the paperwork."

"Do we have clients lined up for these two children?" Danny asked as he fumbled with a Rubik's Cube.

"Yes, we do! The boy will go to Judge Kelly and his wife, the girl will be going to Warden Reynolds and his wife."

CHAPTER FOUR

Inside the county jail intake room, a line of women stood waiting to take their mug shots. Officer Troy operated the camera and called out instructions to the women. "Next! Step up and stand with your back against the wall, say cheese!" She smiled, enjoying her position. Mill stepped up in front of the camera and placed her back against the wall. "Bitch, didn't I tell you to 'say cheese'?"

Mill glared at her.

Officer Troy turned and began speaking to the other women standing in line. "If this skinny-ass bitch don't smile, you ladies will be here all damn night. You can kiss that bologna sandwich goodbye!"

A tall inmate stepped out from the line and said to Mill, "I stink, I'm hungry, and I want to lay down. So, bitch, you better smile before I beat a smile out of you."

Millicent's lips curled upwards in a smile, but her eyes filled with tears. Officer Troy snapped the photo. "Was that so hard? We're all done here, ladies. Now, give me two single lines."

"Where are we going?" Mill asked the officer.

"The Drake, or the Carlton, you choose." Troy and the other officers laughed. "Now, walk through those doors. The ladies on the right, go into the cell on your right. The ladies on the left, go into the cell on the left. Once we get things done, you'll get a bologna sandwich with a juice."

The women went into the cells. Immediately, some began speaking, asking all types of questions, and complaining. Officer Troy ignored them and walked across the area to the lieutenant's desk. The lieutenant, a barrel-chested man in his fifties whom they called "the Godfather," had propped his feet up against the desk. He leaned back in the chair with his eyes closed, and a wet washcloth lay across his forehead.

"I had a hangover this morning that could've knocked out a horse," he said to Officer Troy as she approached him.

"We've got the photos and fingerprints done. We're just waiting on some beds and the doctor."

"Damn," the lieutenant cursed, turning his head in the direction of the inmates, "why the hell are they so loud? If you heifers don't shut the fuck up, you won't be getting anything to eat, Troy yelled." Godfather smirked at Officer Troy. "Well done, officer. How many are there tonight?"

Officer Troy checked the clipboard she was holding. "We have twenty-three, Godfather. And the doctor and nurses are on their way to give them their examinations."

"Hell, I need to be grabbing a few Tylenol from the nurses too, to get rid of this headache."

Mill stood alone in the back corner of the inmate holding cell, trying to make herself invisible, hoping that nobody paid attention to her. Karen Banks, a known inmate in her 30's, walked through the crowd as she stopped in front of Mill. "So, skinny Minnie, what are you in here for?" she asked, looking Mill up and down.

Mill turned away from Banks, sliding down the wall and holding her knees to her chin. "I just want to be left alone," she said, avoiding Banks' eyes.

"Oh, you don't feel like talking about it?" Banks taunted, "You want to be left alone? I get it! I understand." She paused! "But you see, bitch, this ain't no *Little House on the Prairie* shit. I asked you a question," Banks snarled, bending down, pointing a finger in Mill's face.

"If you don't get your nasty-ass finger out of my face, I'll remove it for you."

"Oh! This little bitch got some balls."

"Karen Banks!" Officer Troy called from outside the cell, "Sit your ass down and leave motherfuckers alone before I put your ass in a cell by yourself without food or anything to drink."

"Got it, Ms. Troy," Banks replied, not taking her eyes off of Mill, "and skinny bitch? I'll see you upstairs."

Officer Troy walked toward the holding cell. "Ladies, listen up! I'm going to call your name and when I do, step out of the cell to get your inmate number and see the doctor. Once everyone is done with the doctor, you will be given a uniform with a sandwich and juice. If you're good, I'll think about giving you two sandwiches and two juices each. You're welcome." She paused and waited for a response. "I said, 'you're welcome, ladies.'"

"Thank you, Officer Troy," the inmates mumbled.

Officer Troy walked back to Lieutenant Godfather's desk.

"Any problems?" Godfather asked.

"Nothing to report. I called upstairs, and they have beds ready for them now too."

An officer named Malik approached Troy and the Godfather. "Hi Lieutenant, Officer Troy. We're here for the inmates," she said.

"Great! That means I'm almost done here," Godfather said as he dropped two Alka-Seltzers in a cup of water, drinking it down.

Officer Malik opened a bag full of handcuffs and addressed the inmates. "Hello, ladies! Now, I'm not going to repeat myself. So, please listen up." She pulled out the cuffs and started handing them to the other officers. "I need you all to step out and form two lines. Once you form two lines, you will be cuffed to the person standing next to you. Once cuffed, you will follow the yellow line until we get to the end of the hall. Once there, you will place your clothes in a bag, which will be tagged. You can then change into the DOC uniform that will be provided to you."

"We will have to change without taking a shower?" Mill asked.

Officer Malik stared Mill up and down. "Oh, I see! We have an on the new.

Mill looked down.

"What she in for?" Officer Malik asked Officer Troy quietly.

"Trap housing."

"Trap housing! Oh shit! We have a Nino Brown up in here."

"Funny you say that: her last name is Brown," Troy said.

The officers laughed, and Lieutenant Godfather cleared his throat to quiet the area. "Enough fooling around," he said, standing up with a stack of papers in his hands. "The shift is about to change. I'm taking this paperwork to the captain, and then I'm getting out of here. I need a goddamn vacation." He shuffled away, and Mill watched him leave, her hands shaking at her side.

Officers Troy, Malik, and some others led the inmates into the gym room of the jailhouse.

"Okay, ladies! When you hear your name, you're going to step into the gym and show the officer the number on your hand. Once you show your number, a plastic bag will be given to you. When you get the plastic bag, go stand on the gym floor behind a line of black tape."

"Finally! Hell, I'm tired!" Banks muttered.

An officer called out names, and as each woman heard theirs, they grabbed a clear plastic bag and moved to stand behind the black line.

"Okay, now! Strip!" Officer Malik ordered.

Mill looked around confused as the other inmates started undressing.

"Skinny Minnie, you heard what she said. STRIP!" Banks said to Mill.

"Banks! I don't need you doing my job. Just because you come in and out of here like it's a revolving door doesn't give you the right to talk to my inmates like you're the one wearing this blue shirt." Officer Malik stepped up in front of Mill. "And you..." she looked Mill up and down, "You're a skinny little something. If you're on that dope, you're in for a rough night. Ain't none of that shit up in here."

Mill stared down at the floor. "But new or not," Officer Malik continued, "I said strip!"

Mill unzipped her black jeans and took them off. Slowly, she pulled off her white t-shirt and stuffed it into the clear plastic bag. Officer Malik, who was walking up and down the gym floor, waved her hand in front of her nose and said, "Y'all some smelly bitches. Put your clothes in the plastic bag and set them in front of you so my inmates can come collect them." She gestured for the two female inmates sitting on the gym benches to grab the plastic bags and put them in a rolling bin. "Now, on the count of three, you all will grab your ass cheeks and squat and cough. If you heifers got anything stuck up in your nasty asses, that ass is mine, and your ass is going to the hole. Now, when I say so, open them funky-ass butt cheeks, squat, and cough."

The ladies looked at each other, embarrassed. Officer Malik smiled cruelly. "One, two, three. Squat and cough!" she said, walking around the gym floor as she watched the ladies. "Hold it!" she said suddenly, stopping in front of Mill. She took a half step back to stand between Mill and an inmate with blonde braids. "We're missing a cough," she said to the blonde.

"I coughed," the inmate said.

"Bitch, that wasn't a cough. Skinny Minnie, show this bitch how to squat and cough." Mill squatted and coughed again. Officer Malik focused back on the inmate with the blonde braids. "If you don't stop playing with me, I'll beat the cough out of you."

The inmate coughed lightly. "There! I coughed," she said.

35

"Last chance, bitch," Officer Malik said menacingly.

The inmate coughed louder. Two small bags of dope came falling out of her ass and onto the ground, and she cursed. "Shit!"

"Bingo!" Officer Malik shouted. "I knew it! I know an undercover fiend when I see one." She took a blue plastic glove out of her back pocket, shook it to loosen it, and put it on. Then she picked up the two bags of dope. "Bag this and add a possession charge to Ms. Blondie's paperwork," she said to one of the officers on the gym floor, "I'm sure she'll be sick without this shit too."

Officer Malik dropped the dope into a plastic bag that the other officer held out. She started pacing in front of the women who were still naked. They tried to cover themselves with their hands, except for inmate Banks, who stood up straight with her hands placed defiantly on her hips.

"I don't know about you, C.O.s," Officer Malik said, "but I think this was the best strip show we've seen all week!"

CHAPTER FIVE

It was nighttime in the Ross home. Dae stood at the Giallo Fiorito granite island bar and poured herself a glass of Château Pape Clément red wine. Her husband, Lawrence Ross, came up behind her and kissed her neck. He was a broad-shouldered man in his 50s.

"I see you pulled out the good wine," he said, rocking her gently from side to side.

"Indeed I did," Dae smiled.

"Are we celebrating or trying to forget about a bad day?"

Dae poured a double shot of Johnny Walker whiskey. "Here's your drink, honey."

He took the glass of whiskey from her, and they both sat down at the table. She lifted a plastic bag stuffed full of takeout boxes for her husband to see.

"What do I smell?" Lawrence sniffed.

"They put an I-57 rib joint downtown, so I stopped and grabbed some rib tips, wings, coleslaw, and fries."

"My God, Dae, what are we celebrating?"

Dae walked up behind Lawrence, rubbing his shoulders sensuously. She squeezed them and kissed the side of his neck. "Our new investment we're about to cash in on. But first, I'm going to go check in on Jean and the girls. You enjoy your drink, and I'll be back in a few minutes."

"Hurry back, baby! I'm hungry and horny." He grabbed his manhood, holding the bulge in his hand.

Dae set her wine aside and walked into the den. She walked over to a Shin Kwangho painting hanging on the wall and flipped it on its hinges to reveal a safe. She opened the safe and took out a small black leather bag. She went outside, got into a black Jeep Wrangler parked in the driveway, and drove off.

The cabin was the only source of light or noise when Dae's Jeep pulled up to it, standing in the middle of nowhere. Inside, the five-bedroom cabin house was elegantly decorated and stocked with luxury. c Jackson, a woman in her late 20's, lounged on a white Bond Chesterfield sofa and scrolled through her phone. She wore black leather pants, a black crop top, and red-bottom black high heels.

"Good evening, boss," she said when she saw Dae.

"Hi Jean, how are the girls doing?"

"The girls are doing fine. They're excited about the party and the money they're going to make."

"This is for the party," Dae said, setting the leather bag on the coffee table in front of Jean and revealing its contents.

"Oh, the girls are going to love this," Jean said as she looked into the bag.

Dae sat down on the sectional across from Jean. "Some of the judges' powerful friends will be joining us. One owns a casino, and I'll point him out when he arrives. Make sure you take care of him yourself, Jean."

"Mmm... Casino!" Jean said, looking pleased.

Dae pulled out a marijuana vape from her jacket pocket. "Oh, and Dr. Kook will be joining us as well. Make sure Carmen takes special care of him." She took a hit of her vapor and blew the smoke into the air. "There's a bonus in the bag for you, too, along with money for the midwife. Make sure the midwife stays with the pregnant girls at all times. I want them happy, at least as much as possible. We now have buyers for all of them from overseas."

Jean pulled out a roll of money from the bag and smiled at Dae. "They're all ready to pop any minute now. And I'm pretty sure they'll be glad to get paid."

"I'll see you later," Dae said. She ran her hand down Jean's arm.

"Looking forward to it," Jean replied.

Dae smiled at her and licked her lips. "Remember, I want the girls happy, not sloppy."

* * *

Lawrence laid the ribs, chicken wings, and fries out on the table when Dae returned. "I may not be in the hood anymore, but I love me some I-57 BBQ." He grabbed the mild sauce, pouring it on the food.

"I half expected all the food to be gone by the time I made it back."

Lawrence picked up a rib and bit into it. "Nah, I wanted to wait on you, love, so that we could talk. So, what's the news with the girls?

"Things are going as planned. I took the dope and money to Jean, and she said the pregnant girls are due any day now."

"I will admit, baby, this was the perfect house to buy, and the cabin makes it even better for our business. I'm happy you talked me into it."

"I'm glad I talked you into buying it for us, too. So, did you get the case for Ms. Brown?"

"Yes! I also assigned her a public defender who I got in my pocket." He chewed on his rib.

"Great! The sooner this case is over, the sooner we all get paid."

CHAPTER SIX

T he jail deck door buzzed open, and Officer Snell escorted five inmates onto the deck. The women wore orange DOC uniforms. They stood in the enclosed, locked doors while Snell looked over their paperwork.

"We have five," she said to another officer, "Three on the new and two repeaters. Ms. Banks, you just can't get enough of this place. But it looks like you'll be shipped off to Logan on Wednesday for picking up another case and violating your probation." Then she said to the other women, "Okay, ladies, when you hear your name called, you'll be given your room numbers. Please walk to your assigned room. You'll have five minutes to wash your funky asses. As a heads up, the water only stays hot for three minutes."

The women's names were called out, and they were each handed a package containing a small bar of soap, a toothbrush, a roll of deodorant, a towel, and a gray wool blanket.

"If you need any underwear," Snell said, "let us know, and we'll get you a pair. If you need pads, let one of us know, and we'll provide you with some."

It was after midnight when Mill entered the cell she'd been assigned to, clutching her care package. Inside cell 747, her cellmate, an older white woman in her 40s, sat on the bottom bunk, doing a crossword puzzle. Mill entered the cell, not sure of what to do or say. The woman looked up at Mill but continued to chew the rubber tip of her pencil, lost in thought. "I'm Jazzy, and I recommend you shower now. The water will be cold in a few minutes."

"Yeah, the officer mentioned that," Mill said as she scanned the small cell.

"When the doors pop in a few hours, all the other girls will come out for breakfast, and if you haven't taken a shower, they'll talk about your ass like you're a stray dog."

"Thanks for the warning, but I want to shower."

"You have four minutes before the water goes off," Officer Snell called out from the deck.

Mill hurried downstairs to the shower. Despite the water still being warm, she shivered. She leaned her forehead against the shower wall and let the water run over her back. Then she began to sob.

"Ain't no need to be crying now, skinny bitch. This not even real prison yet," Banks laughing sarcastically at Mill.

Mill turned to look at her. "If you know so much, when do I get to see a lawyer?"

"Are you paying for a lawyer?"

Mill kept silent.

"No money, no lawyer," Banks shrugged and turned the water off.

"Oh, I'm going to get out of here. This some bullshit." Mill said as she rinsed off the soap.

"Yeah, that's what they all say. You're just like the rest of us broke-ass hoes up in here. Lawyer or not, you'll be taking that bus ride with the rest of us to the big house, Ms. Traphouse!" Banks laughed.

* * *

Mill was still asleep when Officer Snell popped open the inmates' doors with a loud clang. "Rise and shine!" she called out to them. Jazzy jumped out of bed and threw on her DOC pants and shirt. Mill laid in bed, facing the wall. abc

"Hey, did you get any sleep?" Jazzy asked her.

44

"No. Not really."

"It's breakfast time. Are you coming out?"

"Do I have to?"

"No, but today they're serving French toast and eggs, and you'll be going to bond court today."

"What's going to happen to me?"

"You have court a few hours after breakfast. If you get lucky, they'll give you an I-Bond, and you can get out tonight. Do you know what your charges are?"

Mill sighed. "The police raided my apartment. They found drugs and guns that didn't even belong to me."

"So, they're probably not going to give you an I-Bond. You have anyone who can post bail for you if you have to pay a bond?"

"I don't have no one who can post my bond. My mother died, and I never knew my dad, and this is my first offense."

"Damn! Sorry about your mom. What happened to her?"

"She died from complications of diabetes right before I had my daughter."

Jazzy looked at Mill sympathetically. "No priors, huh?" She said thoughtfully, "that might work in your favor."

"She don't know what she's talking about," Banks said from the doorway. Jazzy and Mill turned to see her standing there.

"The judge is going to bury your skinny ass," Banks said.

"You could keep it moving," Jazzy snapped.

"You have children, right? You won't be seeing them anytime soon. The way they keep motherfuckers locked up in here. This place is a money mine."

"Oh, I see you one of those wanna-be jailhouse lawyers," Jazzy looking Banks up and down.

"I'm not making this shit up! The prison gets paid for every bitch up in here. Especially us black bitches."

"Hello?" Jazzy responded, "I'm white, and they got me in here too."

"Human collateral, bitches." Banks said and walked away.

Mill looked like she was going to be sick.

"Don't listen to her, Mill. She doesn't know what the fuck is going to happen. I'm going out to breakfast before the food gets cold. Are you coming?"

Mill shook her head. "I don't have an appetite."

"I'll bring you a piece of fruit," Jazzy said, leaving the cell and closing the door behind her.

CHAPTER SEVEN

"Look, detective, I gave you what you wanted. When will I get my cut and get the fuck out of here?" Lou asked Detective Romano, who had just walked into the men's holding cell he was sitting in.

"You'll get your cut," Romano said nonchalantly.

"How fucking long will that take?"

"Don't act like you're brand new to this shit. You'll get paid." Romano grabbed Lou on the shoulder, smiling darkly. "I see you do anything for money. Setting your girl up."

Lou shrugged Romano's hand off his shoulder. "It's not like she's my baby momma or my bitch."

"Woman or side piece, your thirsty ass would've turned in your own mommy. *Culo di cagna!*"

"Yeah, whatever the fuck you just said. Look, I just want my money and to get the fuck out of here so, make that happen, detective."

Detective Romano pulled his cell phone from his pocket.

"Yeah, this is Romano. Lou will be out in a few. Give him what we talked about." He hung up the phone. "You'll be out in a few hours. Go to the spot, and you'll receive half of your package. You'll get the other half once you testify in court. "

"Just let me know the court date, and I'm there," Lou said.

* * *

The next day, a newly-free Lou walked up to the Rothschild liquor store. A thin older man sat on the side of the store selling loose cigarettes out of a black backpack. He took a sip of his Dimitri gin and eyed Lou.

"What up, Charlie!" Lou greeted him, "Let me get a pack of those squares."

"What's good, Lou? I heard them boys popped you and Mill off yesterday."

"Man, them motherfuckers ain't have shit on me. I'm Big Lou! Plus, I got them dirty motherfuckers right where I want them."

"Mhm, so where Mill at?"

"I don't know! I'm just getting out myself."

Charlie pulled a pack of cigarettes out of his backpack.

"Ten dollars for the squares, nigga."

"Damn nigga, ten dollars?"

"You can go your ass up in the liquor store and buy a fifteen-dollar pack from them high-ass motherfuckers in there. I'm going to sell mine regardless. Niggas always trying to be on some cheap shit."

Charlie stood and began to pace back and forth, sipping on his half-pint of gin. "Loose squares!" he called out to a passer-by.

Lou reached into his front pants pocket and pulled out a ten-dollar bill. "Here nigga! Now, give me my squares."

Charlie unzipped the backpack and grabbed a pack of Newport 100s, passing them to Lou. Lou opened up the pack of cigarettes, lighting one up as a dark sedan rolled slowly, bumping NWA's "For the Love of Money."

"Damn, who bumping my shit? That was my song back in the day." Charlie said as he bobbed his head to the beat of the music.

"Your old ass! But them niggas was the shit. Especially Eazy-E and Ice Cube. Now, who the fuck in this car, though. That motherfucker riding low," Lou said as he stared at the car. "Oh? What the fu—!" Lou yelled as three loud bangs erupted.

Gunfire exploded from the car, and Lou was shot in the chest. He staggered and dropped to the ground. Charlie ran into the liquor store as the dark sedan screeched off.

CHAPTER EIGHT

The crime scene had been taped off by the time Detective Romano arrived. Two squad cars blocked off part of the sidewalk and road. Detective Shaw was squatting over Lou's dead body lying in a pool of blood.

"What do we have here, Shaw?" Romano asked.

"It was not his week."

"What are you talking about?" Romano, sounding dumbfounded.

"We hauled this guy in yesterday for possession. Louis Epps. Remember him?" Shaw pulled the sheet back, revealing Lou's face.

"Yeah, we just released him a few hours ago."

"Cigarette Charlie was out here...."

"Did he give you a statement?"

"Nah, he says he didn't see anything. He just ran in the store."

"In broad daylight. Like always, no one never sees shit."

"Definitely not a robbery," Shaw said, "he still has his new Jordans on, and these boys are going for about $500 on the streets."

"Could've just pissed off the wrong person."

"I'm thinking drive-by."

"But the witness didn't see a car."

"He *said* he didn't see anything but do you see these tire marks?" Shaw pointed at the black skid marks.

"They could've been here for weeks."

"Nah. These are fresh." Detective Shaw said. "Hey!" He called out to the crime scene technician, "make sure to snap these tire marks and measure them."

Detective Shaw moved over to the storefront and started inspecting a bullet hole. Romano bent down to look at the tire marks on the road. "Fuck," he said quietly to himself. Then he walked to his squad car and pulled out his cell phone. He looked around to make sure no one was near him, then he said quietly into the phone, "It's done. Man down!"

CHAPTER NINE

Inside the county courthouse, Mill stood with her public defender as the judge read her paperwork. He looked unimpressed. "Child endangerment, gun possession, drug distribution, assaulting an officer, resisting arrest," he read out loud. "The district attorney's office is seeking the maximum sentence of ten years. In light of this and the defendant's gross negligence and history of drug use, I'm labeling her a flight risk. No bond."

"What? A flight risk?" Mill protested, "I never even been on a plane. I don't have a passport. Can I please get an I-Bond?"

"Please escort the inmate out," Judge Kelly said, hitting his gavel on the table.

"What about my kids?" Mill started crying. Two female officers tried to lead her out of the courtroom. "That wasn't my shit! What about my kids?! What about my kids?!"

"You should have thought about them before you turned your home into a dope house."

"You can't do this! You can't do this!" Mill cried, struggling with the officers as tears rolled down her face.

* * *

The door buzzed open, letting the inmates back in. Jazzy was sitting on her bed, eating chicken ramen noodles out of a milk carton. "That's not a good look," she said when Mill entered their cell. Mill slid down against the wall, held her face in her hands, and began to cry.

"They denied me bond, saying I was a flight risk too, and this is my first time getting locked up."

"Damn! That shit ain't right," Jazzy said. She slurped up a mouthful of noodles.

"That bitch this morning was right," Mill said.

"She's just like any other wannabe jailhouse lawyer, Jazzy said as she chewed on the noodles."

"They said I was running a dope house, and my baby girl had dope in her system."

"Was you hitting that shit when you were pregnant?"

"No! Never. I messed around with it, but that was after my daughter was born. There's no way she had anything in her. Hell, I stopped breastfeeding her after she was about two months. She was biting the shit out of my nipples. She's five months now. Whoever did my baby girl test messed it up."

"Yeah, that's fucked up," Jazzy agreeing, with her mouth full of noodles. Some juice from the noodles dripped down her chin as she talked.

Just then, Banks approached the cell with another tall inmate behind her. "I heard they denied your bail. Like I said, you'll be on that bus to the joint too. Bitch, that's going to give us a lot of time to get to know each other. It's not like you'll be seeing your children any time soon."

Mill sprang at Banks and grabbed a handful of her hair before slamming her against the brick wall.

"Oh shit!" Jazzy shouted, jumping up. The noodles spilled all over the floor. She pulled out a toothbrush from a small cut in her mattress that had been carved into a shank. "Stay out of it," she warned the tall inmate, "or I'll shank your tall giraffe ass where you stand."

"Ah, shit!" Banks said, holding her head. She had blood on her hands.

"Bitch, you have one more time to say any-motherfucking-thing about my kids, and I will kill you." Banks, was bleeding from a cut above her eyebrow. She limped away, helped by the tall inmate before any guards noticed what was going on.

"Damn Mill, I didn't know you had it in you like that. You flop-bopped that bitch!"

Mill went over to the sink and wet her face. "She had it coming. I'm so tired of that bitch. She been talking shit since I got here."

Jazzy grabbed a roll of tissue and started cleaning up the noodles. "I'm glad you beat her ass." She paused. "But, uh, you owe me a pack of ramen noodles."

Mill looked back at Jazzy, and they both laughed.

"Thanks for having my back," Mill said. "Now, where in the hell did you get a shank from?"

"Look, I'm in here for stabbing my children's father up. If these bitches wanna get out of line with me, I got something for them." Jazzy spun the shank in her hand like a professional drummer before stuffing it back in the mattress.

"Damn. You stabbed your children's father?"

"I killed that bastard. I'm still here because my lawyers are trying to get me off on a self-defense plea."

"Why you stab him?"

"I mean, if somebody is on top of you, choking the shit out of you, what would you do?"

Mill shook her head in disbelief. "You had a knife, and he still came at you like that?"

"It wasn't a knife I used. He had me on the floor choking the shit out of me. All I could think about were my two boys. That's when I saw a pair of scissors on the ground, so I grabbed them and stabbed him in the neck. I had all types of orders of protection against him, but he wouldn't leave me alone."

"Two boys!"

"Yeah! They're with my mom and family now until this court shit is over. Once I'm out of here, I would love to take my boys to Disney World for a week or two."

"Hell yeah, I've heard it's nice. Maybe one day we'll take our children together." Mill wet some tissue and used it to wipe the blood off on her hand. "That bitch Banks is going to try to pull it again, I bet."

"I wouldn't be so sure," Jazzy said, "she might be trying to hide them knots you just gave her ass."

They both laughed.

* * *

Five months later, Mill sat before a jury of eight men and four women to receive her sentencing. The judge on the case was Lawrence Ross, Dae's husband. "Counselor," he said, "have you spoken to your client about her sentencing?"

"Yes," the counselor responded.

"Ms. Brown. Did your lawyer explain to you how this will go?"

Mill fidgeted in her chair nervously. "Yes," she answered shyly.

"Well, since you opted out of having a jury trial and having a bench trial instead, and from the evidence presented in the case, I sentence you to ten years for child endangerment, gun possession, and drug distribution."

Mill broke down in tears as two female officers led her out of the courtroom.

CHAPTER TEN

It had been a month since Mill's sentencing, and the Rosses were having another party in their cabin. They sat in a corner drinking champagne and watching the escorts entertain their guests.

"Honey, the evening is going great, and our guests are enjoying themselves, as always," Judge Lawrence Ross said.

"They better be, for the fortune we're paying these girls," Dae answered.

Judge Ross turned his wife so that she was facing him, and then he kissed her. "You're doing wonderful, honey." She kissed him back, biting his lower lip and looking up into his eyes. He was about to kiss her again when Dae turned away to nod at a guest.

"And I see our new hotel mogul is enjoying himself too," she said.

"Why wouldn't he be? Jean knows how to make anybody feel good. We both know that." The couple smiled suggestively.

"Yes, she does," Dae said, licking her lips and watching Jean. Jean was perched on the arm of a couch, nibbling the hotel mogul's ears and rubbing his small hard dick. "Look who's coming our way."

Warden Reynolds had walked up to the Rosses.

"Howdy, Judge. Mrs. Ross."

"Aw, Warden Reynolds. Enjoying yourself?"

"As always, Judge."

"We're sorry you didn't make it to the last event," Dae said.

"Yeah, work keeps me sometimes." Warden Reynolds lowered his voice and leaned into the Rosses, passing a thick vanilla envelope to Judge Ross from the inner pocket of his suit jacket. "But I got it squared away. Are we all set to go now? Here's the cash."

"Rest assured, you and your wife will be getting your baby," Judge Ross said. He looked at the money before putting it inside his tuxedo pocket.

"The paperwork for the child is being put together now," Dae said. "Once that is complete, you and your wife will be holding your new baby girl."

Warden Reynolds grabbed Judge Ross by the shoulder. "Great! My wife will be thrilled. Remember, she just thinks this is an adoption."

One of the escorts, Carmen, approached them. She smiled softly as she wiggled her finger at Warden Reynolds.

"I see Carmen is waiting on you," Judge Ross said, "enjoy the rest of the night, Warden. We'll talk about this later."

Warden Reynolds walked towards Carmen, wrapped his arms around her waist, and followed her into a room.

A tipsy Detective Romano wobbled towards the Rosses. "Nice party, Your Honor," he said.

"Detective! Glad you made it. I see you're feeling good."

"I assume that means the job is all done?" Dae asked the detective.

"It's done. I just need to cross some I's and dot some T's." Romano pulled out a flask of tequila and drank from it.

But uh, I need that money now. I have bills to pay and mouths to feed.

"Patience!" Judge Ross said, "You're going to get your money."

"That could be... when is that?"

"As my husband said: patience, detective."

"C'mon. It's not like you don't have the cash. I saw the warden pass you an envelope."

"Detective, you better sober up real quick, or I'll be having one of my security take you home." Judge Ross looked over at a tall, muscular Rick Ross-looking man wearing a tight all-black tuxedo. Detective Romano swallowed his drink and nodded. He grabbed a finger sandwich from a passing server and walked off.

The next morning, Jean walked into the Rosses' kitchen and poured herself a cup of coffee. Dae was sitting at the table with Mr. Fluke.

"Sorry, I didn't know you had company," Jean said.

"It's okay, Jean. Mr. Fluke was just stopping by to drop off some documents."

"Hi Jean, you're looking beautiful this morning," Mr. Fluke said, smiling flirtatiously at Jean.

"Thank you, Mr. Fluke."

"Please, call me Danny."

"You got it, Danny."

"Well, *Danny*, thank you for dropping these off," Dae said, gesturing for him to leave. Dae walked Mr. Fluke to the front door.

"Enjoy your day, ladies." Mr. Fluke left, getting into his Audi Q8.

"Now that's one weird dude," Jean said as Dae walked back into the kitchen.

Dae laughed softly. "He's loyal, and you know he has a crush on you."

"You, out of all people should know, he's not my type. I don't care what type of car he drives or how much you pay him." Jean walked up behind Dae and kissed her back as she said this. She reached down and caressed her breasts. "You miss this?" She whispered as Dae moaned. "Your wet pussy tells it all."

The judge walked out of his bedroom and looked over the victorian staircase. The sight of the two women made his dick hard. "Well, that's a pretty picture to wake up to this morning," he said as he stroked himself gently. The women turned around and looked up at him. "How about you too come up here and join me. "

CHAPTER ELEVEN

M ill brushed her hair in front of the plastic mirror hanging on the wall of her cell.

"You're up early, girl," Jazzy said as she got out of bed to go sit on the toilet seat. She was wearing only a t-shirt and a pair of white panties. "What time is it?" She asked, pulling down her panties and sitting on the maxi pad-padded stainless steel toilet.

"It's 3:45 Mill said, still brushing her hair. Officer Snell will be popping the doors at 4:00 for breakfast. So, I figured I'd eat and shower early since they'll be coming to get me around 6:00 am."

Jazzy yawned again and said sleepily, "Yeah, get a shower in before they cut off the water." She got up and flushed the toilet. Mill stood aside from the silver steel-mounted sink so Jazzy could wash her hands. "I might as well stay up with you and take me a shower too. My lawyer is coming to see me today."

"Yeah, you were telling me last night, but my mind was somewhere else, and I dozed off."

"It's cool. It's good that you got some sleep. You were knocked out! I remember when you first got here month's ago. You were a little dope-sick, but you got past that shit real quick."

"Like I said before, it was just some shit I was trying after me, and my daughter's father broke up. I was more of a pothead than a dope fiend."

"Your hair looking nice, Mill. "I'm going to miss you. Hopefully, I'll be getting out of here, and you can look me up whenever you get out." Mill walked up to Jazzy and hugged her. Jazzy returned the hug with an affectionate smile. The cell doors buzzed open, and Mill and Jazzy grabbed their towels and soap.

"Good morning, ladies!" Officer Snell called out from the deck, "for those of you who have court today, please make sure to take your showers after breakfast."

After showering, Mill and Jazzy sat with their food trays at the silver picnic-like tables nailed to the deck floor.

"Pancakes and eggs?" Jazzy said, cutting into a flat pancake with a plastic fork. "And they're hot? I'm shocked!"

"I don't remember the last time we had some hot breakfast," Mill agreed.

Inmate Banks walked towards them with three other inmates in tow.

"The bitch walking this way," Jazzy said quietly to Mill.

"Here we go," Mill said.

Jazzy looked over at Officer Snell, who sat in the deck office. "Don't let this bitch fuck your day up."

Banks leaned in towards Mill, lowered her voice, and said, "Look, Brown, when we get to the joint, you know the big house, watch your back on the yard. Ain't going to be no C.O's there to protect your skinny ass." Banks smacked Mill's plate off the table, and it clattered to the ground.

Officer Snell looked up from her desk in the shielded office and shouted, "Hey! Someone better clean that shit up!" Banks walked away as the three other inmates followed her.

"I guess I might have to put these paws on her ass again, but the next time, it won't just be a little bleeding." Jazzy smirked, and Mill picked up the tray, cleaning up the spilled food.

"Logan's a pretty big place," Jazzy said, "maybe you won't even see her. Or maybe you'll be on a different deck than her."

"We'll see! Regardless, I'll be ready for that bitch."

Later that day, Mill stood in line, shackled to the other inmates as an officer called out their names and numbers. The inmates had to repeat their information before getting on the bus.

PART TWO

(Present Day)

CHAPTER TWELVE

T wo FBI agents walked into Warden Reynolds' office at the women's prison.

"Hello, agents," Warden Reynolds started saying when he saw the men, "what can I do for you?"

"Warden, I'm Agent Shaw, and this is Agent Porter."

"How may I help you guys? Is this about one of my inmates?"

"No," Agent Shaw said.

"Warden Reynolds," Agent Porter said, "do you know a Judge Ross?"

"Yes, I know Judge Ross. What is this about?"

"Is this your wife and child in this picture?" Agent Shaw pointed at a picture frame on the warden's desk.

"Yes, that's my wife. What-?"

"Your wife Emily, correct? Pretty picture," Shaw interrupted.

"Again, may I ask what this is about?" Warden Reynolds asked impatiently. "Why are you asking me questions about Judge Ross and my wife?"

"How old is your daughter, warden?"

The warden leaned back in his chair with a look of confusion on his face. "I'm going to ask again, why the hell are you here?"

Agent Shaw tossed a file onto the warden's desk. The warden looked at it nervously. "What is this?" He asked, opening the file. Inside were pictures of Judge Ross, Dae Ross, Dr. Kook, Detective Romano, and the warden himself.

"What do these pictures have to do with me?" The warden stuttered.

"Immunity!" Agent Porter responded.

The warden took a deep breath, swallowed nervously, and placed his hand on his forehead. He rubbed it slowly, staring hard at his desk.

"Agent Porter, I believe the warden got his answer to why we're here," Shaw said. "We know Judge Ross and his wife are selling children and running an illegal prostitution ring and providing your prison with inmates."

Warden Reynolds' forehead glistened with sweat. He licked his lips nervously. "I don't know what you're talking about," he said.

Agent Shaw sat up straighter in his chair and slammed his hand down on the warden's desk.

"I'm going to tell you just what we're talking about. In order for this prison to keep running, you need inmates. We know the judge provides you with inmates by incarcerating women and giving them a long sentence, even with petty crimes, so you can still receive funding for this prison."

Agent Shaw leaned back in his seat, lowered his voice, tilted his head, and said, "For every inmate that comes into this prison, you're getting paid. We also know that you bought the baby girl in that photo with you and your wife. Not only that, but we have recordings and evidence of you supplying inmates from the prison to parties for Judge Ross and other high rollers."

Warden Reynolds stood up, walked over to the window, and looked out at the female inmates in the yard. He turned around to face both agents.

"I would like to talk to my lawyer," he responded softly.

Agent Shaw and Agent Porter stood up. "Aw, he's lawyering up," Shaw said.

"You have twenty-four hours to be in our office with your lawyer, Mr. Reynolds." Agent Porter pulled his wallet out of his back pocket. "Here's my card! Twenty-four hours."

"If you're not in our office within that time frame, a warrant will be issued for your arrest. Have a nice day." Agent Shaw smiled sarcastically, putting his hands in his pockets as he and Porter begin to walk out of the warden's office. At the door, he stopped, turned around, and looked at Warden Reynolds. "Oh, and by the way, we spoke with your wife. We didn't have to say much for her to start singing like a canary to save her own ass. Like my partner said, "Twenty-four hours, Mr. Reynolds."

* * *

Later that day, Agent Shaw and Agent Porter walked through the Fox Valley Mall, following Jean as she talked on her cell phone carrying shopping bags.

"Girl, yes, I'll be there in a little bit to get my hair done. Make sure you have that wine I like. I'm about to go in the food court and grab me something to eat, a sister hungry. I'll see you in a few." Jean hung up and walked to the elevator door. She pushed a button and got in. As the elevator doors started closing, Shaw and Porter stepped into the elevator, standing behind her. Jean looked at them suspiciously, adjusting her hair and outfit. She scrolled through her phone, which was chiming with notifications.

"Ms. Jeannette Jackson?" Shaw said.

Jean turned around, put her cell phone in her pocket, and looked at the men. "Do I know you?" she asked, her eyes narrowing.

"No, you don't know us, but we know all about you."

71

"Ms. Jackson, can we have a few words with you?" Agent Porter asked, pulling back his navy-blue blazer displaying his FBI badge. The elevator doors pinged open.

"And what is it that the feds need to talk to me about? I pay my taxes."

"Let's sit," Agent Shaw suggested, "and I will explain it to you."

Jean walked over to a table in the food court. She placed her shopping bags on the chair next to her as the agents sat down across from her. "Again," she asked, "what is this about? And how did you know I'd be here at the mall?" She crossed her legs and fumbled with her phone.

"You wouldn't believe the things we know about you, Ms. Jackson. Things like your favorite salon, the salad you order for lunch, what type of gas you put in that cute little car of yours, and the prostitution ring and money laundering." Agent Shaw said.

Agent Porter passed Jean a folder. Jean's eyes widened.

"Where did you get these pictures? I don't run a prostitution ring. I work as a manager for an escort service. And money laundering, I don't even know what that is."

"So I guess you don't know about the baby-selling, neither?" Porter asked.

Jean breathed in deeply, squared her shoulders, brushed her hair out of her face, and gave the agents a small, tight smile. "Like I said, I manage an escort service. Not a day-care center."

"And like we said," Agent Porter countered, "we know more than you think we know. And if you want to ever see your mother and daughter – who you visit every month in Nevada – I advise you to cooperate."

Jean looked at the two men, inhaled lightly, and folded her hands on the table.

"I'm listening," she said.

CHAPTER THIRTEEN

M ill and her cellmate were shooting hoops on the basketball court that afternoon in the jailyard.

"Okay, we're going to play a game of H-O-R-S-E, and the loser has to wash the winner's uniforms. Including socks and underwear too, okay, Remi?"

"Okay, I'm in! But Mill, I don't wash no other woman's underwear but mine. So, you have to wash them yourself, baby girl. That's if I lose," Remy said.

The two started shooting the ball at the rim one at a time. Mill and Remi laughed and joked, taunting each other as they continued to shoot baskets. Just as one shot was about to go in the hoop, inmate Banks walked up with three other inmates and caught the ball as it bounced off the rim.

"Oh, look who we got here. Didn't think you'd see me again, huh, Brown?"

"What the fuck do you want, Banks? As you can see, we're playing a game here," Mill said.

Banks bounced the ball then kicked it. A few other inmates looked on at the commotion.

"Oops. I don't give a fuck if y'all playing a game or not."

"Mill, who the fuck is this bitch?" Remi asked, arms crossed over her chest, eyeing Banks up and down.

"Bitch, you don't know me. I will drop your Remy Ma-looking ass." Banks displayed a shank from under the side of her pants. "Jazzy is not here to protect you now."

"Bitch, I didn't need Jazzy then, and I don't need her now. I beat your ass before, and I'll do it again. I'm not that same Brown you knew when we were in the county."

"We'll see about that, bitch," Banks said, rushing at Mill with the shank.

"If you bitches think about jumping in," Remi said to the other girls, "you're going to be some shanked bitches too." She pulled a shank out of her sock, tossing it to Mill. "Now y'all even!" Remi said.

Other inmates quickly surrounded Mill and Banks.

"Bitch, you want to play dirty, bring it. You fat-ass bitch." Mill said.

Banks rushed at Mill with the shank, tripped her up, and threw her to the ground. "Bitch, I'm going to make your face unrecognizable."

Mill and Banks tussled. Banks straddled Mill, trying to stab her in the face. She landed a cut across Mill's forearm.

"Bitch, you're trying to fuck my face up? Nah, I'm not going to let that happen." Mill flipped Banks on her back and began to punch her repeatedly, blood gushing from Banks' face.

The yard siren began to sound loudly, and Mill threw Remi the shank. Remi took it and walked off with other inmates.

"What the fuck is going on over here?" A yard officer called out.

"I was playing a game of H-O-R-S-E, and Banks comes walking up to me talking about some shit that happened in the county jail a while ago. She pulled a shank out on me. The same shank she's hiding in her pants leg there on her right side."

"Is that true, inmate Banks?"

"She attacked me!" Banks yelled. "That bitch got a shank too!"

The yard officer walked over to Banks, pulling the shank out of her pants. A second officer patted Mill down and came up empty-handed.

"I told them not to let you out the hole! It looks like you'll be going back for a while."

The yard officer informed the other officers to clear the yard and get the inmates back to their rooms. She escorted inmate Banks to the hole.

* * *

Twenty-four hours later, in the FBI building, Warden Reynolds entered an interview room with his lawyer to talk with Agents Shaw and Porter. The four of them sat at the table.

"Hi, I'm Mr. Reynolds' Lawyer, Counselor Pasch. My client told me bits and pieces of what's going on, but please explain so I may get a sense of the matter?

"We have evidence that your client has been taking in inmates to get illegal funding from corrupt officials, and he has been provided inmates through Judge Lawrence Ross sentencing them to his prison. Not only that, the baby girl that your client and his wife have was sold by Judge Ross and his wife and bought by the warden." Shaw explained.

Counselor Pasch looked over at Warden Reynolds.

"And what evidence do you have against my client to accuse him of the things you say he committed?"

Agent Porter placed a folder in front of Counselor Pasch. He examined the evidence before leaning over to whisper to his client.

After a moment, Pasch cleared his throat. "If my client agrees to help you get the bigger fish, what does he get in return?"

"Immunity for his testimony and a new start in life. This story will be going live on every news channel. We suggest you cover your ass, so you and your wife can move on from this."

The warden looked down at his hands folded on the table. When he spoke, his voice shook.

"What about my wife? And what about our baby girl? Do we get to keep her? We're the only family she knows."

"Well, your wife claims she had no knowledge of your criminal activities with Judge Ross and hired her own lawyer. As far as the baby girl, she'll be going back to her mother."

* * *

In the Rosses' home, the Rosses were in bed watching the evening news. Judge Ross rubbed his fingers along Dae's thighs softly. "A few more weeks, my love," he said, "and we will be drinking mojitos in the Caribbean. I can't wait! Nude beach here we come," Judge Ross said, climbing on top of Mrs. Ross. He put his dick in her wet pussy, and she moaned. The news announcer came on with breaking news.

"Just in. A woman has been a victim of another carjacking that turned deadly. The victim, twenty-six-year-old Jeanette Jackson, was getting into her car when two males approached her to carjack her Mercedes Benz. The victim was shot once and pronounced dead on the scene."

"Boy, this pussy feels good every time I'm in it." Judge Ross said, but Dae had suddenly pushed him off her. She sat up, alarmed.

"Wait, Lawrence, did you hear what the news announcer just said?" She got out of bed, grabbed the remote control, and hit the rewind button.

The news announcer came on again and repeated the news, and Dae began to cry hysterically. "That's Jean!" She started putting on her gown, robe, and slippers, as the judge stared at the television, frowning in disbelief.

"These gang bang motherfuckers here in Chicago don't give a fuck whose life they take," he snapped. He got out of bed and walked over to Mrs. Ross to console her. "Dae, I will find out who did this."

"I have to go to the cabin to talk to the girls," Mrs. Ross said, grabbing a duffel bag full of money from the closet.

* * *

Later that evening, Mrs. Ross walked into the cabin and placed the duffel bag on the floor. The girls were all weeping and consoling each other. "I take it that you ladies saw the news," Dae said. She walked to the bar and poured herself a shot of vodka. She downed it quickly, then poured another, emptying that one as well.

Her hands shook. "This is tragic, what happened to Jean, and trust me, we will find out who did this and hold them accountable," she said as she paced the floor.

"She was just going to get her hair done and do a little shopping," Carmen said, with tears rolling down her face.

"Look, the cops will be coming around, I'm sure, to ask a lot of questions. We will have to shut down until we can find out what happened with Jean and I can get things in order. I'll make sure you are compensated, but for now, you all have to leave." The girls disappeared into their rooms and started to gather their belongings. Carmen stayed behind talking with Dae.

"You all have thirty minutes," Dae uttered. "Jean was my best friend. Carmen looked at Dae as her eyes begin to fill with tears. I'll call her mom and let her know what happened before the police do. I just can't believe they killed my girl. Yes, call her mom and make sure the girls are all out, and this place is clean spotless. Here's five thousand dollars each for them. Ten thousand for you, and seventy-five thousand for Jean's mother and daughter. It will help with Jean's funeral expenses. I'll call Jean's mother after things have calmed down."

Dae passed Carmen the duffel bag and smiled sadly. "I know Jean meant a lot to you, and you two were like sisters. I loved Jean, too. She meant a lot to me as well." The two women hugged and cried. "Thank you for all your help, Carmen. I will reach out to you once this blows over.

CHAPTER FOURTEEN

In the women's prison holding cell, Agent Porter and Agent Shaw watched on as Mill, horrified, looked at the pictures in the cream-colored folder.

"This is Lou," Mill said, placing the picture down on the table.

"Yes, Louis Epps! Someone killed him in a drive-by shooting."

Mill looked at the agents, shocked. "I didn't have anything to do with that. I don't know anything about a drive-by. I been in here locked up, but you guys already know that, right, Agent Shaw?"

"Ms. Brown, can you tell us who else you recognize in the photos apart from Mrs. Ross and Lou?" Agent Porter asked.

Mill looked back at the pictures. "This is Dr. Kook. He's one of the doctors at the Woodlawn clinic." Mill placed the pictures down one by one as she recognized the faces. "And this is Detective

Romano. He charged me with possession with the intent to distribute and gun charges, but you already know that, too." Mill placed the picture down, her voice rising with anger and resentment. "And this is Judge Ross, the man that took my freedom away." She looked up at the agents with a blistering frown on her face. "I answered your questions. Now, can you tell me what's going on?"

"Let's just say a lawyer will be coming to talk to you about a new trial." Agent Shaw said.

"New trial about what? Why would I be going back to trial?"

"We'll be seeing you shortly," Agent Shaw replied, getting up. Agent Porter joined him, and they both walked out as the corrections officer escorted Mill back to the deck.

At the deck, Remi was sitting in her bunk, writing a letter when Mill walked in. "That was a long visit. So who was it?" She asked curiously.

Mill grabbed a carton of grape juice sitting in the cell window before sitting down beside Remi. "Girl, that was the FBI," she said with a serious look.

"The feds! What the hell did they want with you?"

"I don't know, but they were asking me questions about my DCFS caseworker, my doctor, and Lou."

"Lou! The dude that got popped off with you?"

"Yeah," Mill said, "and now he's really popped. He's dead."

Remi leaned back against the wall and put her pen and paper down. "Damn! Do they think you had something to do with it?"

"Nah. I was in here when he got killed. They say it was a drive-by."

"So if it wasn't about Lou, what they want?"

"I don't know. They showed me some pictures asking me if I knew the people in the photos."

"What photos?"

"It was a photo of my DCFS caseworker and the judge who sentenced me. They also showed me a photo of the detective that raided my apartment and a photo of one of the doctors I use to see at the neighborhood clinic. They said I'd be having a new trial, and I should be expecting to hear from a lawyer soon."

"And what's the new case about?"

"I don't know," Mill said, agitated. Remi patted Mill's knee to comfort her.

CHAPTER FIFTEEN

J udge Ross and Mrs. Ross sat at a table in a posh banquet hall, sipping wine and engaging in conversation with the other well-dressed people who sat with them. It had been months since Jean's death, and now that things looked like they had blown over, the Rosses were back to hosting and attending lavish parties. That evening, they were attending an awards ceremony held to honor Lawrence.

Judge Kelly, dressed in a sharp black tuxedo, walked onto the podium and took up a microphone. "May I have everyone's attention?" he said, tapping the mic. The crowd quieted down, and all eyes turned on him. "As you, all may know," he continued, "Judge Ross has done a lot while serving the courts for over thirty years. He's put away bangers and felons. He is also responsible for putting the program 'Battle Through' together, a program that helps children who were victims of gun violence get scholarships to attend college."

The crowd applauded as Judge Kelly continued. "Judge Ross is not only my colleague, but my friend, and I'm proud to present him with the William H. Rehnquist Award."

Judge Ross stood up and kissed his wife as the crowd rose to honor him. He walked up to the podium and shook hands with Judge Kelly. "Thank you all for the applause. Please be seated. First, I would like to thank my beautiful wife, who has put up with me for all these years. I would also like to thank my colleagues for nominating me to receive this award. Without you guys, this wouldn't be possible."

Agent Shaw and Agent Porter walked into the room, and Judge Ross faltered when he saw them. A worried look crossed his face, and immediately he replaced it with a nervous smile.

"Judge Ross, can you please step down and come with us?" Agent Shaw asked.

The crowd had started whispering, and the worried look had come back on Judge Ross's face. He took a step backward, not sure what to do. "I'm in the middle of my speech. May I ask you what this is about?"

"Let's not do this the hard way; please step down." Agent Shaw replied.

"No! What is this about?"

"Alright then, let's do this the hard way," Shaw said, walking up to the stage. He grabbed Judge Ross by his arm and cuffed him just as Agent Porter took Mrs. Ross' arm and gestured for her to get up. "Judge Ross, you are under arrest. You have the right to remain silent." Agent Shaw read Judge Ross his rights as photographers took photos of the judge getting handcuffed and escorted out.

* * *

The trial for the Judge and his wife begin three months later. Agent Shaw was the first witness to be called. The Bailiff swore him in before he took the stand. The district attorney addressed him after. "Agent Shaw. Can you tell me how long you and your team have been investigating Judge Ross and his wife?"

"The judge and his wife have been under our investigation for a little over two years now."

"And why so long?"

"We had to make sure we were following the right leads and protocols, and we were gathering evidence to build a case."

Judge Ross was sitting next to his attorney. He fumbled his fingers as he listened. Sweat glistened on his forehead.

"We were tipped off about the judge through an informant, whom the judge thought of as a friend."

"And what did this informant tip you off about?"

"We received word that the judge was sending folks to jail for a long time due to false arrests. We also learned that the judge and his wife were running an illegal black market operation."

"And what did this black market sell?"

"They sold children who were placed into the DCFS system."

Judge Ross shook his head and mumbled under his breath. His attorney gave him a warning nudge, and he sat up, a frown on his face.

"And when you say 'system, can you explain to the court what you mean?"

"They were working with a dirty detective to get women on low income with younger children arrested."

"And what happened after the arrests?" The district attorney asked as he looked over at the jury.

"After the women were arrested, their children were then placed into the DCFS system, which was overseen and ran by Judge Ross wife, Dae Ross. The children were then sold to people looking to buy them for human trafficking, slavery, or for those who just couldn't have children on their own."

"And is it true that Judge Ross and his wife also ran a whore house or, as they say, an illegal prostitution ring from their guest house?"

"Yes."

The district attorney dismissed Agent Shaw, and Judge Ross's attorney cross-examined him before he stepped down from the stand. Marco Romano was the next witness to take the stand. Romano, dressed in an orange DOC suit, was handcuffed and escorted in by two federal officers.

"You were once known as Detective Romano, who use to work for the Chicago Police Department, correct?"

"Yes," Romano answered.

"Did you also work for Judge Ross?"

"Yes."

"And what did you do for the judge?"

"I made illegal drug busts on single women's homes in order for their children to be placed in the DCFS system and sold on the black market.

"I'm done with this witness," the district attorney stated as he looked at the jury. Romano was escorted back to the holding cell after the judge's attorneys had cross-examined him.

Hours into the trial, District Attorney Young said, "I would like to call my next witness."

A woman walked into the courtroom. She wore red high heels, a tight black fitted dress, and oversized black sunglasses that covered her face. She took the stand and waited. Dae, who was sitting behind her husband, did a double-take and turned around to look at the witness.

"Hello, ma'am. Can you please give the courtroom your name?"

The woman took off her glasses. Underneath, she had big, beautiful hazel eyes. "My name is Jeannette Jackson," she mumbled her name softly as she cleared her throat.

"And Ms. Jackson, can you tell me how you know the Rosses?"

Jean gazed over at Judge Ross and Mrs. Ross. She looked sad and apologetic. She gave them a small smile before turning to look back at the district attorney.

"I worked as their madam, among other things." The jury looked on, surprised at this revelation.

"And when you say you were their 'madam, can you explain to the court what a madam does?"

"I ran girls for them. If a man or woman needed a nice date or a good fuck, I'm the one who made the arrangements."

"So, basically, you ran a prostitution house."

Jean looked down at her hands folded in front of her. Her voice was low. "If that's what you would like to call it," she said. The people in the courtroom had begin to whisper. The judge hit his gavel on the table to quiet them.

"How many years have you worked for the judge and his wife?"

"About five years."

"Did you also witness the judge and his wife accepting money for children to be sold?"

"Yes," Jean replied.

"Were you also involved, romantically or sexually, with the judge and his wife?"

"Yes."

"During your time as their madam, how many children would you say the Judge sold on the black market?"

"I believe fourteen. I have evidence of where every child was sold and who they were sold to. I also have the names of all the political figures who visited the cabin weekly to sleep with my girls."

"Were some of these girls underage?"

"Yes."

"Were you paid to tell the court anything you just mentioned under oath?"

"No! I'm telling the truth. I just want a new chance to move on with my life."

Judge Ross and his wife exchanged shocked glances.

"I'm done with this witness," Attorney Young said. Jean stepped down from the dock, walked past Judge Ross and Dae, hesitated in front of them, and said, "I'm sorry." Then she walked out towards the courtroom doors where Carmen was waiting for her.

"I would like to call my next witness to the stand: Mr. Reynolds."

Mr. Reynolds walked into the courtroom, and the bailiff read him his oath.

"Mr. Reynolds, how long were you the warden at the penitentiary?"

"About fifteen years."

"And how do you know Judge Ross?"

"Through mutual friends."

"Let's cut to the chase. Did you buy a baby from Judge Ross and his wife?"

Warden Reynolds hesitated, not making eye contact with the Rosses. "I... we..." He stuttered.

"Mr. Reynolds, did you buy a baby from Judge Ross and his wife?"

"Yes," the warden answered quietly.

"And how much was this child worth?"

Warden Reynolds looked up at District Attorney Young. "My wife can't have children," he said softly.

"The question was, how much did you pay for the baby girl?"

"One hundred thousand dollars."

The district attorney dismissed Warden Reynolds from the stand, saying he had no more questions for him. The judge on the case hit his gravel. We'll hear closing arguments now. An hour later, the jury had reached a verdict. A foreperson passed a piece of paper to the bailiff, who passed it to the Judge. The Judge took a peek at it and gave the piece of paper back to the bailiff, who returned it to the foreperson.

"We, the jury, find the defendant, Mr. Lawrence Ross, guilty of child trafficking, running a prostitution ring, and wrongfully incarcerating people," the jury read.

"There is no need to drag this on any longer as far as sentencing," the judge on the case said, "Judge Ross, I find what you did to be truly disgraceful. You make other judges and our entire justice system look bad. Because of you, we may have lawsuits on our hands. Placing people in jail for your financial gain is despicable. Selling children to be slaves or to become part of a sex trafficking ring is immoral." Dae begins whimpering in her chair.

"I hereby sentence you to twenty-five years which you will start to serve immediately as of today."

"Get him out of my courtroom," the ruling judge said. Dae tried hugging her husband before he was led out of the courtroom but was told to take a seat by the officers.

CHAPTER SIXTEEN

"Inmate Brown, you have a visitor," a corrections officer called out to Mill. Mill walked out of her room towards the officer.

"Who is it?" she asked.

"I think it's a lawyer," the officer replied. She took Mill to a small holding room. Once she was inside the room, a tall, well-dressed white man walked in. He was wearing a blue suit with a red tie and a crisp white shirt. He held a brown leather briefcase.

"Hi, Ms. Brown!" He extended his hand out to Mill, who took it slowly, shaking it uncertainly.

"I'm Attorney Mackey. I will be helping you get your children back."

"How will you be able to do that? I'm in here...?"

"As of today, you will be released due to some new evidence."

"The evidence the feds were talking about?"

"Yes. Regarding Judge Ross and his wife. You'll get to see your children again as part of the lawsuit. ?".

Mill eyes got bigger. "Lawsuit?!" she asked.

"Yes, lawsuit! You were set up and wrongfully accused by a judge who was married to your DCFS worker. They also had the doctor you were seeing lie, saying your baby girl had drugs in her system. The warden has been fired, and Detective Romano is also serving time for the hit he placed on Lou Epps. Mill looking in disbelief. And what about the crooked judge and his wife? What the fuck happened to them? They both received a lengthy prison term.

Mill stood up. Tears formed in her eyes as she placed her hand on her chest. "Wow! So, all of them were working together? I don't believe this shit. So, I really get to leave this place and get my babies back?! Yes, you get to leave this place. And this lawsuit?! I want to sue them all. The Judge and that Chinese-looking ass bitch. The Department of Children and Family Services and the Chicago PD.

"And that's why I'm here," Mackey responded. "I'm going to make sure you get what you deserve."

Mill could not control her tears anymore as they flowed like water. A moment later, she broke out in large sobs. Then she suddenly got up and hugged Mackey.

"Your children are there now, waiting to see their mom. Congratulations, Ms. Brown."

EPILOGUE

"Hello, I'm calling for a Jasmine Pearl. My name is Mill. Is she available?" She smiled as a familiar voice came through the line.

"Bitch, I was wondering if you would ever call me. I saw the news. Them was some dirty motherfuckers," Jazzy said. Mill sat back in her new home and watched her children play as she listened to Jazzy's voice on the phone. She was happy. She had started a new life with her children and, after receiving a two million dollar settlement from the state, she had gone back to school and received a bachelor's degree in business management.

"I see you beat your case too," she said to Jazzy.

"Yeah, I'm free!"

"We're free! And I just wanted to call and say thank you, Ms. Pearl, for helping me through."

"I told you everything was going to work out. So, what are your plans now?" Jayden walked up to Mill and reached out to her to be picked up.

"Well," Mill said, "I remember you telling me that you had two boys around my kids' age and with all we been through, I thought we could go to Disney World."

"Stop playing, Mill! Yeah, my kids may be a little older than yours, but so what? They'll still have fun. Hell, I'm going to have fun. Much needed!" Jazzy said excitedly.

"I'm not playing Jazz. Hell, I got money now, and I'll be paying for everything, so you do not need to worry about shit."

"I know that's right! And you deserve every penny with the bullshit our so-called justice system put you and me through. Well, are your kids okay?"

"The kids are fine. They seem happy just to see me and be with me. I bought them a dog, and my son is in love with him. They're playing now."

"Well, that's good!"

"I'm buying this building in Englewood that will help young women with day-care, employment, domestic abuse, and drug counseling. It feels good to be clean and not putting that shit up my nose anymore. I want to help others going through the same thing I went through. Then, I also thought about you and your situation."

"Which one?" Jazzy laughed.

"The pain you went through with your children's father and the stabbing. I thought you could come on as a counselor since you have a bachelor's yourself. I thought you could share your story to help other women get out. Of course, you'll get trained by staff."

"So, it'll be like the group sessions we had in the county?"

"Yes! And some one-on-ones. I've been researching it. I'm teaming up with another non-profit that's fighting for this same cause, as well as community pastors and city alderman's who will be helping me get this off the ground."

"Okay, I see you been busy. And Mill, I'm proud of you: especially about not putting that shit up your nose. You're a smart girl. The Lord gave you a second chance and gave me a friend. I'm down to help! So, when do we leave?"

"I wanted to speak with you first to ask what your schedule looks like."

"It looks like I can be packing our shit now," Jazzy laughed. "Thanks, Mill. I appreciate you, and I'm glad God allowed us to meet. Regardless of how we met, I'm glad we did."

"So, we'll talk more about it on the trip. I'll make the arrangements now."

"O-M-G, I can't believe we're going to Disney World," Jazzy said.

"O-M-G, believe it because we're going! I'll talk to you later. I'm about to feed my little ones," Mill said and hung up.

The phone rang just as Mill hung up with Jazzy. Hello, she said. There was silence on the other end. "Hello, I can hear you breathing!"

"Hello," said a voice from the other end, "I'm looking for a Millicent Brown."

"This is she! May I ask whose calling?"

The person on the other end got quiet.

"Okay, I have my children to attend to. I don't have time for prank phone calls." I'm about to hang up.

"Wait, Millicent, my name is Melissa. I believe I'm your sister. My father's name is Willie Brown."

"Sister! Father! How did you get this number? Is this real?" Mill asked in disbelief.

"I hired a private investigator after my mom told me about you, and I saw your case on TV."

"My mom never told me anything about you. I only know that the man she calls my father was in and out of jail, and I don't remember him." Mill explained.

"We have a lot to talk about," Melissa said.

"Yes, we do. And if you're lying and you're trying to get money out of me because of what you saw on TV, that's not going to work."

"I don't need your money. I make six figures a year as a VP for a tech company. I was calling to hear your voice, to see if it's true."

"So, you mean to tell me, I have a sister, and you're her? How do I know if you're telling the truth?"

"I can prove it to you."

"And how are you going to do that?" Melissa went silent. Then a man's voice came on.

"Mill, I'm your father."

Mill sat down at the kitchen table and looked at the phone, confused. Then she spoke into it. "My father?!"

End.

www.ingramcontent.com/pod-product-compliance
Lightning Source LLC
Chambersburg PA
CBHW050545280326
41933CB00011B/1726